·KINGFISHER·
KINGPINS

The Superbook of GYMNASTICS

Brian Hayhurst

KINGFISHER BOOKS

Contents

This revised edition published in 1986 by Kingfisher Books Limited
Elsley Court, 20–22 Great Titchfield Street, London W1P 7AD
A Grisewood & Dempsey Company
Originally published in hardcover by the Hamlyn Publishing Group
in 1980 as *Gymnastics.*

BRITISH LIBRARY CATALOGUING IN PUBLICATION DATA
Hayhurst, Brian
The superbook of gymnastics.
2nd ed. –(Kingpins)
1. Gymnastics–Juvenile literature
I. Title
796.4'1 GV461

ISBN 0–86272–197–0

Cover designed by the Pinpoint Design Company
Phototypeset by Southern Positives and Negatives (SPAN), Lingfield, Surrey
Printed in Hong Kong

Cover: Shaposhnikova of the Soviet Union on the beam
Previous Page: Chinese gymnast Yanhone Ma at the 1984 Olympics in Los Angeles.

Gymnastics

Gymnastics is among the most popular of international sports. At the Olympics, the World Championships, and other events, competitors perform in front of large audiences, and under the eyes of millions of television viewers. Meanwhile, for every well-known international star, there are many enthusiastic youngsters training and competing in their local gymnasiums and schools. This book deals with the many aspects of this complex and challenging sport, from the first exercises performed by the beginner, to the tough routines seen at top competitions. It describes the history of the sport, the complicated rules which govern it today, and the organization required behind the scenes of every event. Colour diagrams and photographs illustrate the different standards of equipment and competition, and explain some of the basic and advanced movements seen at today's events. A gymnast's training and preparation, and her life as a top competitor are also described. Finally, the names and achievements of some champion gymnasts are recorded, together with the results of international competitions in recent years. This book will appeal to all those who are keen on this popular and dramatic sport.

Continental Sports

Since the tiny Olga Korbut caught the imagination of the world with her thrilling performance at the 1972 Munich Olympic Games, women's gymnastics has become a leading international sport. Unlike the straight-faced, controlled gymnasts of the past, Olga showed her emotions – from cheeky grins of delight to tearful desolation. Young girls all over the world suddenly had someone their size and around their age with whom they could identify. Olga could be their older sister. She had, by her brilliant performance, directed interest to an activity which had in the past received little attention. The boys had always had sports in which to win fame and glory – football, cricket and baseball; now the girls had found a sport in which to sparkle at a young age. Suddenly long queues formed outside gymnastics clubs all over the world. Everywhere girls were deciding: 'I want to be a gymnast – like Olga Korbut'. Once the 'cinderella sport', gymnastics has never looked back.

◄ The 1972 Olympic beam champion Olga Korbut captured preparing the chest roll from a 'flying back flip'. Olga was responsible for starting the gymnastics explosion.

► Ludmilla Tourescheva held almost every gymnastics title during her long career, and gained much respect around the world for her calm thoughtfulness as a competitor. Renowned for her 'classical' style, she made few mistakes and performed best under pressure.

The Story of Gymnastics

People first became interested in gymnastics thousands of years ago. In ancient Greece, at the first Olympics in 776 BC, the Greeks stressed the value of exercise systems as a preparation for other events such as wrestling and jumping. Gymnastics aided general fitness.

The importance of physical culture declined with the fall of the Greek and Roman empires. For many centuries acrobats alone kept alive the gymnast's skills.

In 1811 a Berlin schoolmaster, Ludwig Jahn, founded an outdoor gymnastics school, and created apparatus for use there. At the same time a Swede, Pehr Henrik Ling, introduced a different type of gymnastics, based on mass exercise to command, and aimed at developing perfect rhythm of movement. Ling's methods were also adopted for military drilling. The two styles competed for

▲ Boys practise on various apparatus at Ludwig Jahn's outdoor gymnasium. Much of it looks comical today, but the seeds of later equipment can be clearly seen in these early designs.

► This wall painting from the palace at Knossos in Crete shows early gymnasts 'bull vaulting'. When the bull flung back its head, the youth somersaulted over its back to be caught by the girl behind.

popularity.

In 1881 a Belgian, Nicolas Cuperus, founded the Federation of International Gymnastics (F.I.G.) linking the various national bodies. In the 1920s, the federation brought together the precision of the German method and the fluency of the Swedish style in one system.

The excavation of the site of the ancient Greek Olympic games by German archeologists led to a revival of interest in the games. The first modern Olympics were held in 1896 in Athens, and involved 311 competitors from 13 countries. These early athletes were all men. For many years, the thought of women competing in the Olympics was totally unacceptable. Female gymnasts had to wait until the 1928 games in Amsterdam, for their first appearance, when the Dutch team won the gold medal.

The USSR took part in their first Olympics at Helsinki in 1952. In particular, the performances of Soviet women gymnasts were outstanding, and marked a turning point in the history of women's gymnastics. For almost a decade, the Russian Larissa Latynina dominated the major women's events. She won more medals than any other female gymnast, and held many European, World and Olympic titles.

Before 1972, gymnastics had little television coverage. At the Munich Olympics that year, gymnastics gained a world-wide television audience when the Russian Olga Korbut was seen for the first time. Her skill and charm captivated the public, and she became a household name overnight. Suddenly, crowds of youngsters wanted to 'be like Olga'. Gym clubs had waiting lists. Gymnastics had become a major sport.

After Olga, came the astonishing Romanian girl, Nadia Comaneci. Her youth and skill drew attention to gymnastics, and further increased the sport's popularity. At her first appearance in the West, at Wembley in 1975, the 13 year-old emerged as outright winner against formidable opposition.

▼ Although women did not take part in competitive gymnastics until 1928, these Danish women gave gymnastics exhibitions at the 1908 games. By a vote of 15 to 6, the Olympic nations decided to include a modest programme of women's events in 1928.

Elena Shaposhnikova at the 1979 European Championships. Precariously balanced on the beam end, she demonstrates strength, elegance and balance during this split leg, one arm stand. These pictures show how far gymnastics has come since the Danish women gave their exhibition in 1908.

Nadia went on to win numerous competitions, and score the maximum 10 points on dozens of occasions. Demand for her appearance stimulated the Romanian Gymnastics Federation to create better facilities in their struggle for supremacy in the sport. But with gymnastics now attracting millions of youngsters, other nations also began to produce excellent gymnasts, in readiness for the 1980 Moscow Olympics. Sadly, a political row was to keep many countries away from these games.

The Americans, who had been advancing steadily in the world rankings, became serious contenders for a major title in the early 1980s. This coincided with preparations for the 1984 Los Angeles Olympics. Unfortunately, the organizers suffered the withdrawal of nearly all the Eastern Bloc countries.

Although many of the world's best gymnasts were absent, there were dozens of technically brilliant exercises performed at Los Angeles, particularly by the Romanian team, and by the elegant Chinese, who almost defeated the American team.

The extraordianry talent of Maxi Gnank from East Germany and Olga Mostepanova from the Soviet Union remained unseen in the West until the 1985 European and World Championships.

Gymnastics are now so well established that it is certain that they will continue to flourish and attract more people – both spectators and participants.

Olga Korbut on her way to winning the gold medal on the beam at the Munich Olympics in 1972. Olga won a team gold medal, but lost the coveted champion's title, mainly due to an uncharacteristic slip on the bars. Notice the bare wooden beam, since replaced by beams with a special non-slip cover.

Starting Gymnastics

▲ **A gymnast's coach offers physical assistance, encouragement and friendship through the successes and failures of her career. Here the coach is supporting the gymnast and commenting on the parts of this simple 'V' sit position which need to be improved.**

Ideally, girls should be introduced to 'fun gymnastics' at four or five years old. Then, if they decide to take up the sport seriously, they are better prepared for the tough training involved. Details of clubs offering gymnastics are available from the national association or a local sports centre.

Newcomers to a club join a beginner's course in which they do simple exercises in large groups. Those showing ability are tested for entry into regular club sessions. At first, progress seems slow, and the young gymnast is often bored by the emphasis placed on elementary movements. But it is essential to perfect basic movements and techniques at the outset, as these are the foundations of more difficult, and more dangerous work.

Girls who start gymnastics at about six can expect to take part in competitions for up to 15 years.

How to Improve

A gymnast should look after her body. Plenty of sleep, a well-balanced diet and regular exercise, such as jogging, all help improve performance in the gym. She should be on time for all her training sessions, so as to take part in vital warm-up excercises such as group dancing, jumping, running or games.

Another basic aid is the gymnast's diary, in which she records body weight, work done at each session and any changes made in her exercises. At home, she can practise arm and body movements in front of a large mirror, paying attention to head and arm movements.

▲ **This young girl vaulting will feel confident with her coach 'standing in' to give help should she need it.**

The Way to the Top

There are various schemes to encourage young gymnasts. The B.A.G.A. – Coca Cola Awards offer a series of badges and certificates for agility tests. The Gold Top Awards for girls are a little more advanced, offering certificates for work on the four apparatus.

The Harrison Drape Championships enables both boys and girls to perform group floor sequences, together with individual exercises.

The National Development Plan is a series of set movements used in regional and national events. One of the most exciting events for a young gymnast to aim at is the televized Thames Television 'Young Gymnast of the Year'.

▲ Attention to detail has been behind Soviet success in gymnastics. Every Soviet gymnast spends long hours at the ballet barre, learning disciplined movements which will automatically assist technique and extend her range and flexibility, while adding the body control that is absolutely essential on the beam.

◀ Diane Bull during one of Britain's most prestigious competitions, the Champion's Cup at the Royal Albert Hall. Selection for this event is keenly fought among Britain's best seniors, although ocassionally there are juniors who receive their first taste of a big audience at this event.

Equipment

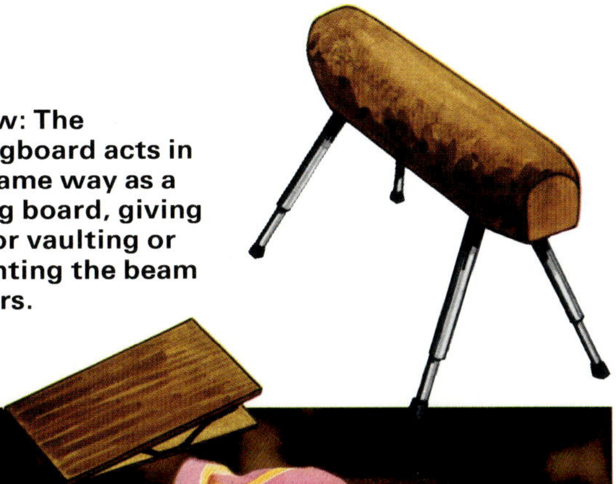

Below: The springboard acts in the same way as a diving board, giving lift for vaulting or mounting the beam or bars.

Left: The approach run to the leather-covered horse must be over 24 m long. A measuring tape at one side helps the gymnast mark out her run up length.

Below: The asymmetric bars were developed in 1951 from the men's parallel bars. There should be an adjustment of up to 1 m between them.

▲ A gymnast completes the first flight of her vault.

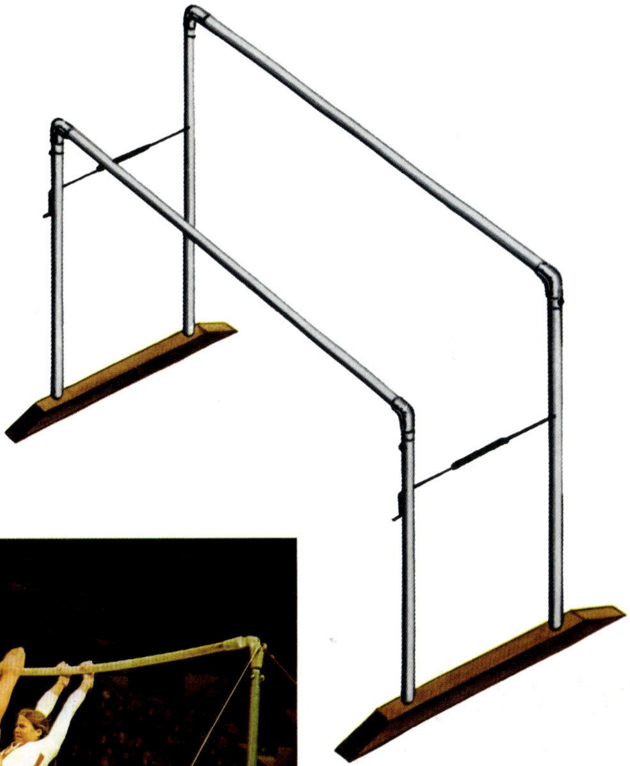

► Ludmilla Tourescheva on the bars.

Below: The balance beam, commonly called the beam, was introduced when women's equipment was standardized at the Helsinki Olympics in 1952. The top of the beam is slightly padded and covered with suede leather, and the beam is held tight to the floor. The tubular base feet are the same depth as the matting which totally surrounds this, and all other equipment at competitions.

► A gymnast on the beam

The Vault

Since ancient times when Cretan warriors used to vault over live bulls, people have always had an urge to test their skill by leaping over an object.

Today, vaulting is an integral part of almost every school P.E. course. It requires little space and gives immediate satisfaction for comparatively little effort.

In senior competitions, the horse is fixed at 1.20 m, but for junior events, the height is usually reduced. Beginners often use the small buck, surrounded by protective matting. The correct execution of basic vaults, that is squats and straddles, is important. Beginners must also be taught to jump correctly and encouraged to run. Sprinting should be part of the training programme.

When vaulting, it is essential to wear gym shoes. A gymnast should never vault in socks or bare feet.

▲ Nadia Comaneci landing after a vault. Judge No 1 is in an excellent position to observe any faults or unnecessary paces.

► Comaneci captured in a daring somersault position, grasping her knees ready to pull them together for a faster rotation.

◀ **The first flight phase: fully extended, body held under tension ready for the impact on the top surface of the horse. Notice the wind stream through the gymnast's hair, giving an indication of her speed.**

Rules for Vaults

Each gymnast is allowed two vaults and the better one is recorded. In many competitions, the two can be identical, but in major F. I. G. events they must be different. In these competitions, the two scores are averaged to give an actual score.

One extra run is allowed provided the gymnast does not touch the springboard; if she does touch the apparatus, it counts as a vault.

Before starting her run, the competitor raises a card showing the number of the vault to be attempted. If the vault performed is not the one indicated, she loses 0.5 points. If she fails to touch the horse, technically she has not made a classified vault, and scores 0. Judges deduct between 0.2 and a full point for faults in technique. For example, poor flight onto the horse loses 1 point; legs bent or apart 0.3 points; bent arms, up to 0.5 points; poor flight from horse, 0.5 points. Similar deductions are made for other mistakes.

In a team competition, only six of the twelve vaults performed by the team may be the same.

Preparation
The gymnast must know clearly what she intends to do before she starts her run, and have checked the equipment.

Approach run
The speed of the approach should increase steadily, reaching its maximum just before the board.

Pre-jump
At this stage, correct arm action – like that used by sprinters in athletics – provides the vaulter with the necessary lift for her vault.

Contact with the springboard
Only the toes and soles of the feet, never the heels, should touch the board. Elasticity is greatest at the highest point in the spring-board's curve. It is this spot the vaulter aims for.

Take-off
Take-off should be fast and vigorous, using the arms to the maximum.

First flight phase
According to the type of vault, this is the point when the body stretches forwards and up-wards and, in the case of an overswing vault, begins to rotate. The arms are fully extended and must remain straight at the elbow.

Second flight phase
The shape of the second flight determines exactly which vault is being performed. Tucking creates a rapid turn, while turning the shoulders, head and arms gives the gymnast a rapid spin or twist. At the end of the phase the body begins to flatten ready for landing.

Landing
The balls of the feet should touch the ground first. Leg and hips are bent to absorb the body's force. Finally, the body is straightened to complete the vault.

Beginners will find themselves doing a lot of vaulting and agility work, since it develops leg power, stamina and courage. It is of great importance that the gymnast is warmed up before vaulting takes place. Remember that the vault is first in competitions, and a good vault is a great morale-booster.

Above: The squat on, jump off vault is one of the first vaults to be learned. Keeping the legs together, the flight on to the horse should not be too fast. The feet are placed together on the vault, and the gymnast immediately jumps to land.

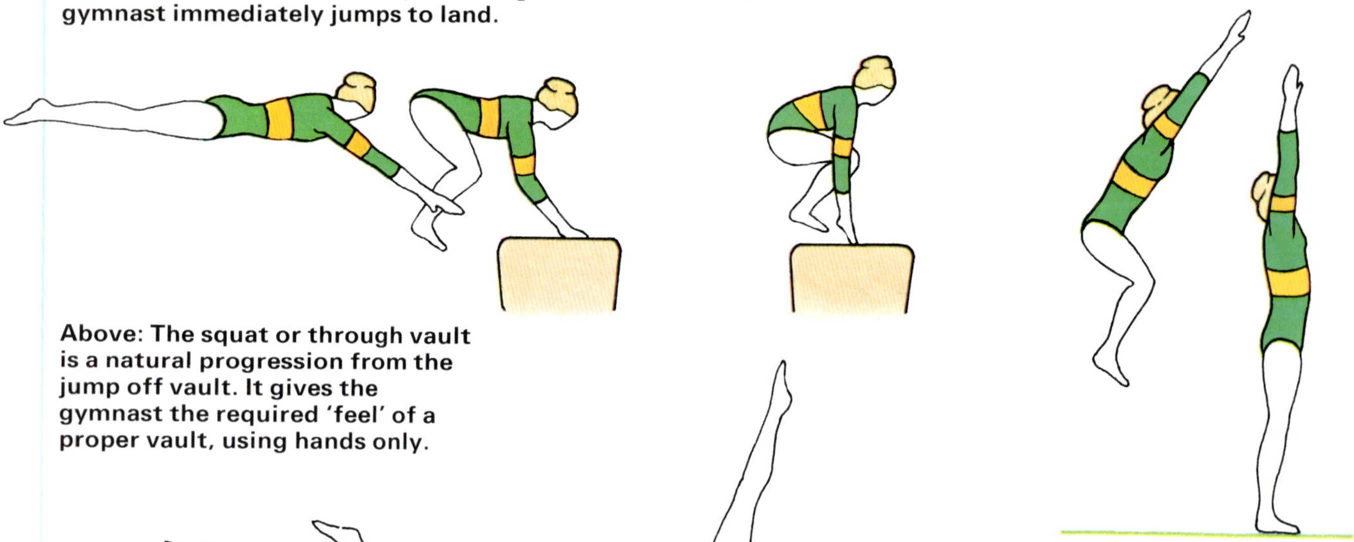

Above: The squat or through vault is a natural progression from the jump off vault. It gives the gymnast the required 'feel' of a proper vault, using hands only.

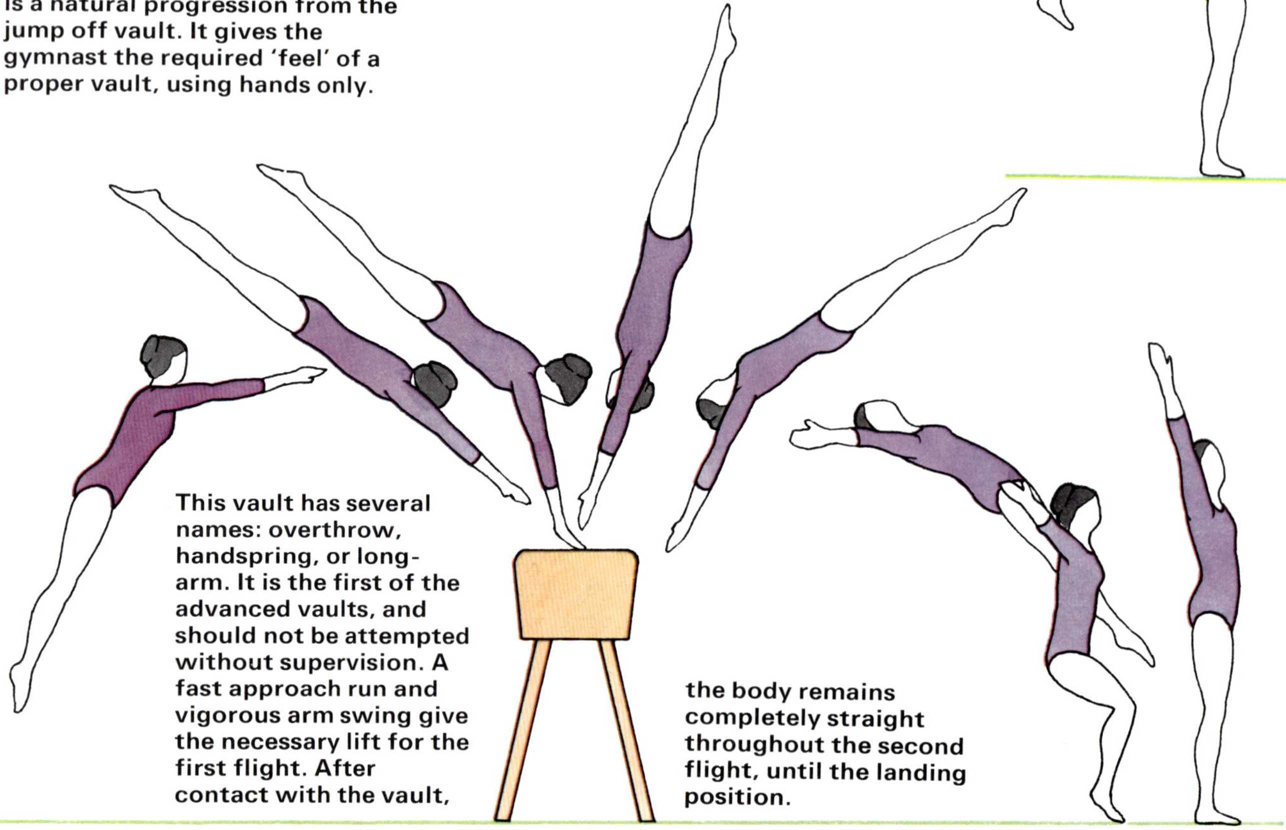

This vault has several names: overthrow, handspring, or long-arm. It is the first of the advanced vaults, and should not be attempted without supervision. A fast approach run and vigorous arm swing give the necessary lift for the first flight. After contact with the vault, the body remains completely straight throughout the second flight, until the landing position.

Below: The Tsukahara vault is named after the Japanese man who invented it in 1970. It became one of the most widely used vaults at top level, by both men and women. This quarter turn on and back somersault from hands is a very difficult vault.

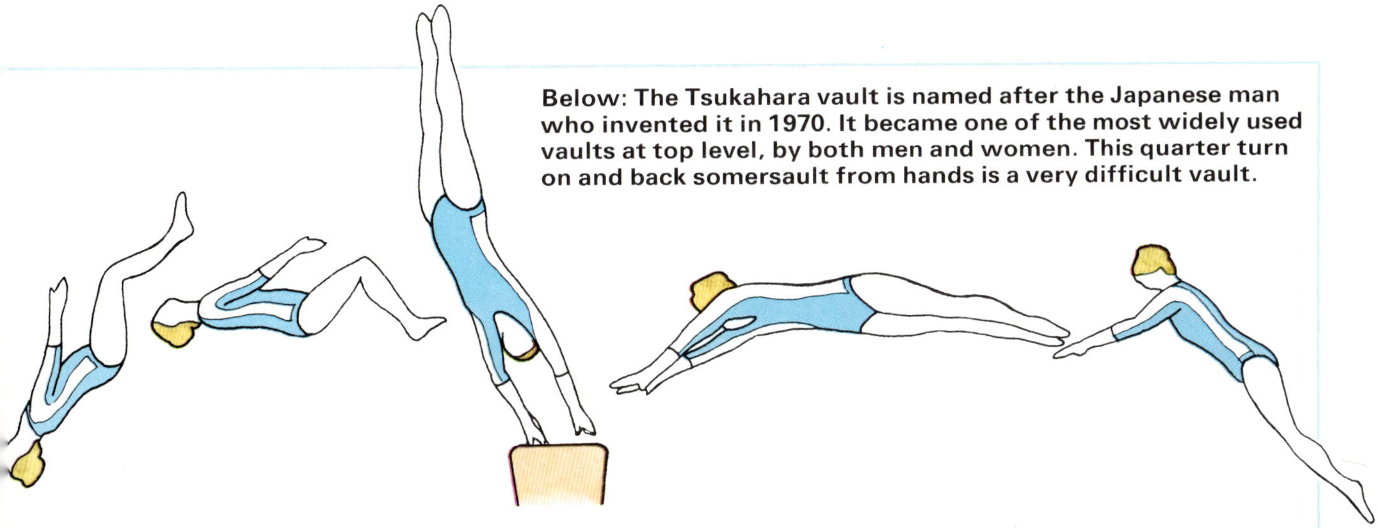

Below: There are 129 registered vaults in the F. I. G. code of points for women, beginning with the straddle vault. Although not a difficult vault, it can be made to look very advanced.

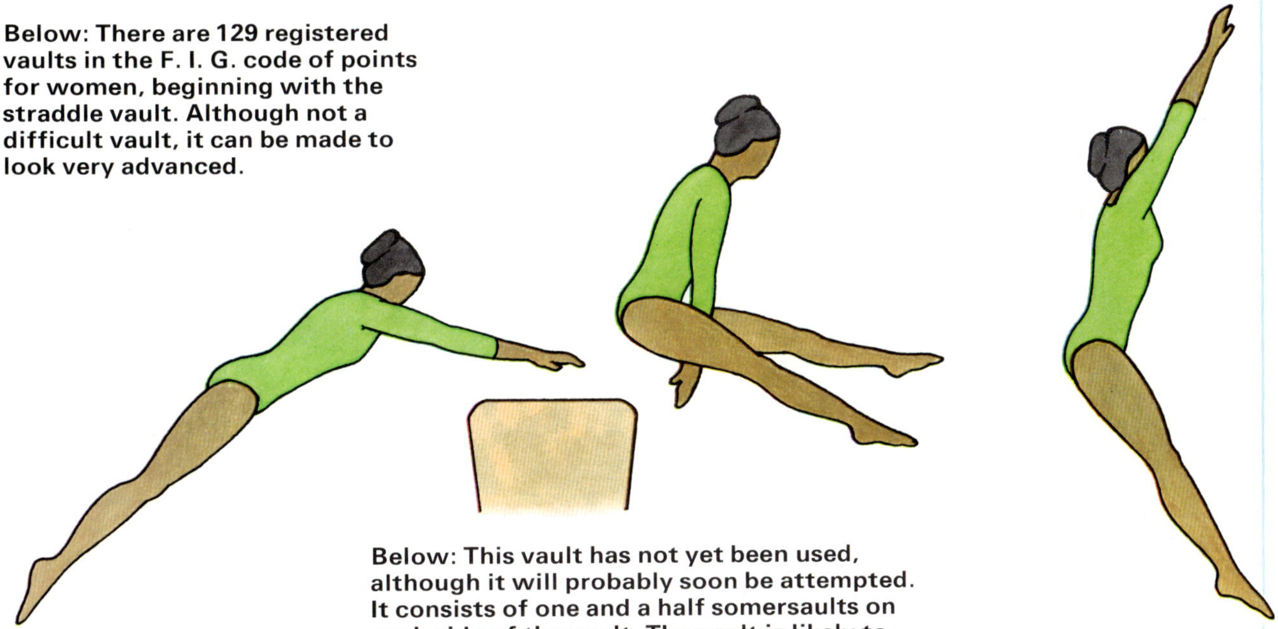

Below: This vault has not yet been used, although it will probably soon be attempted. It consists of one and a half somersaults on each side of the vault. The vault is likely to remain a standard exercise, and vaults to become more and more acrobatic and complex as gymnasts seek to improve their scores.

On the Bars

▲ **The overall Olympic Champion in 1984, Mary Lou Retton, demonstrates an exaggerated position as she fights to achieve a handstand on the bars. She would have been happier with a perfectly straight body.**

► **Olga Korbut demonstrates the importance of having the bars adjusted properly. The bend in the hips should be exactly across the low bar, and the distance between the bars will be different for each gymnast.**

Handchalk

The white powder used by gymnasts on the hands during bar exercises is magnesium carbonate, commonly known as 'chalk'. It can be in small blocks or, more usually, in powder form. Chalk absorbs perspiration and generally improves grip on the bar. There are gymnasts who prefer both their hands and the bars to be completely free of chalk, often moistening them with a damp cloth before they begin. A firm, solid grasp creates confidence when attempting difficult movements.

Young gymnasts find bars the most difficult piece of apparatus, as they lack the arm and shoulder strength needed even for the simplest of moves.

The young gymnast begins bar work by using the lower bar only. She then transfers to both bars. The bars are adjusted to suit each individual competitor by a screw turnbuckle between the uprights. The tops of the gymnast's thighs should rest on the lower bar when she is hanging from the top bar; this allows maximum hip flexion.

To obtain the maximum of 10 points, a gymnast should perform an exercise which contains the required number of what are described as B, C and D moves, correctly linked together.

A good bar routine includes handstands, somersaulting and twisting elements. The gymnast should move smoothly between the two bars, change direction frequently and end with a dismount to an upright stance. There must be no obvious stops or breaks. The

gymnast may begin standing, running, or use a springboard. Handstraps are usually worn for protection. If the straps break, the gymnast is allowed to change them, providing she does so within 30 seconds and re-starts her performance from the very point at which she broke off.

Each time the performer leaves or falls from the bars, an automatic deduction of 0.5 points is made.

Even the most advanced and complex exercises contain some basic movements similar to those learned by a beginner in her early days. Such fundamental movements must be properly mastered, under the guidance of an expert coach.

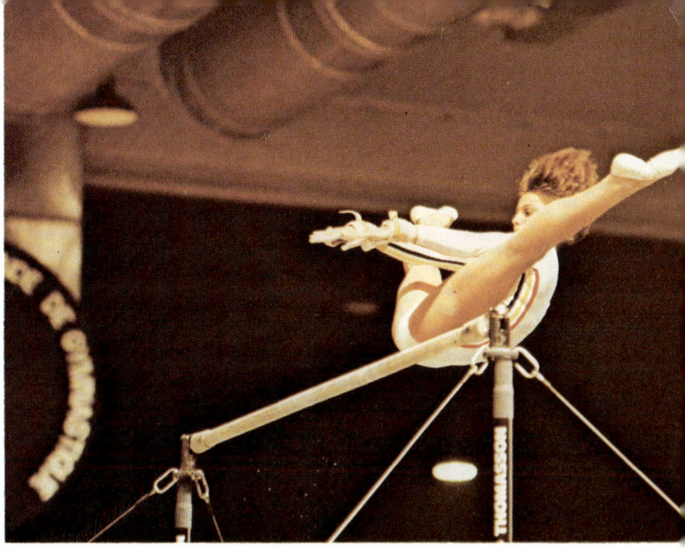

▲ **Nadia Comaneci about to re-grasp the bar following her remarkable straddle front somersault. This was a movement invented by her, and first performed at Montreal in 1976.**

◄ **Erika Zuchold captured in mid-flight. In 1970 this East German gymnast achieved her best result, coming second to Ludmilla Tourescheva in the World Championship.**

▼ **This gymnast will lose marks because she is about to land with her ankles apart.**

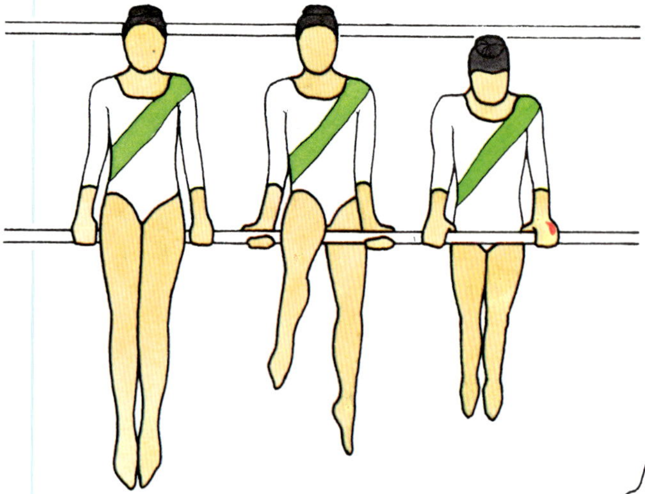

Above: The three basic support positions. In the back support (left) body weight is taken partly on the thighs and partly on the arms. The Mill support (centre) is used for beginners to circle the bar, a movement known as a Mill circle. The front support (right) is the position most frequently used by gymnasts on bars.

Above: The lay up or beat from support. From front support, the legs are swung backwards after lowering the body. The shoulders rise as the legs are lifted and arms straighten.

Above: The underswing dismount from standing is a movement which appears easy, but which may take a long time to master. It is of great value in later gymnastic training. The move requires the shoulder swing to be delayed as long as possible, and then the feet shot up high. Once learned, an extra half turn can be added to the movement.

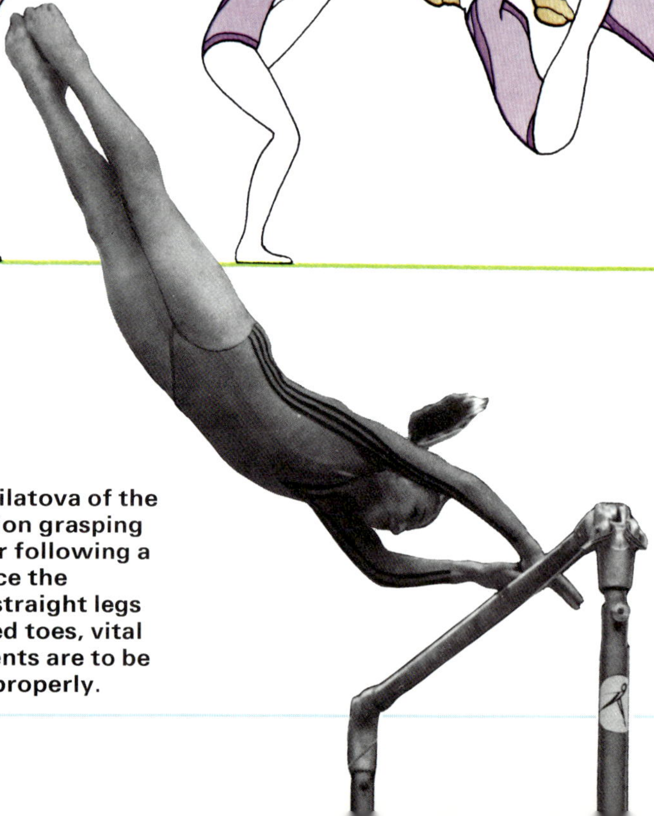

► Maria Filatova of the Soviet Union grasping the top bar following a turn. Notice the perfectly straight legs and pointed toes, vital if movements are to be executed properly.

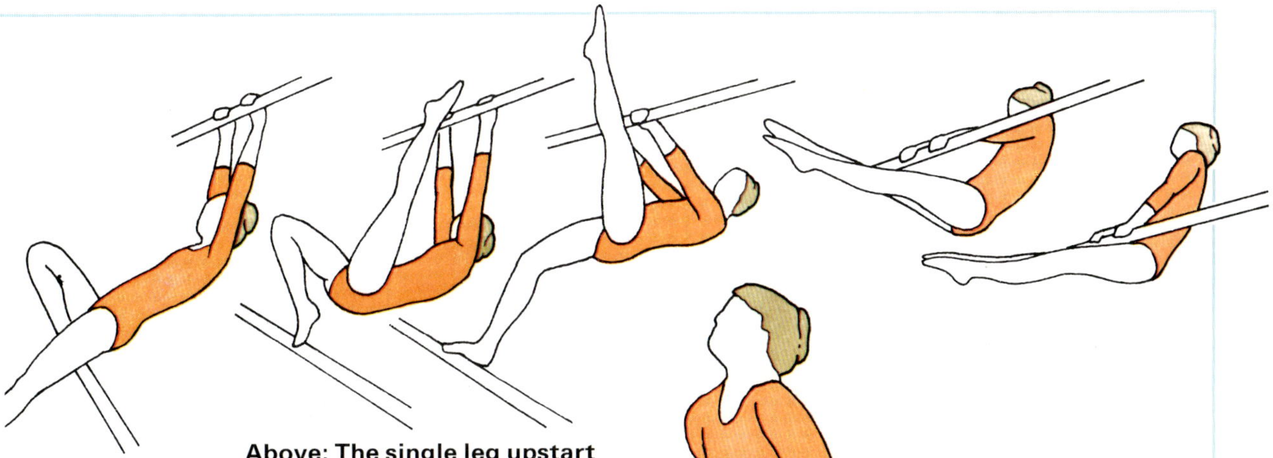

Above: The single leg upstart (from standing on a low bar) is a movement which will be much used as the gymnast becomes more advanced, when a modified upstart with two legs is used.

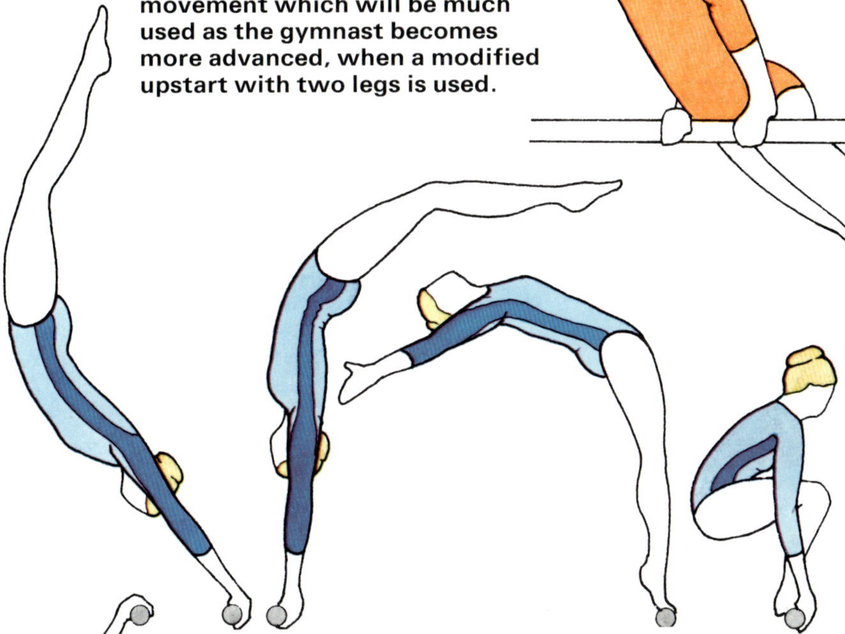

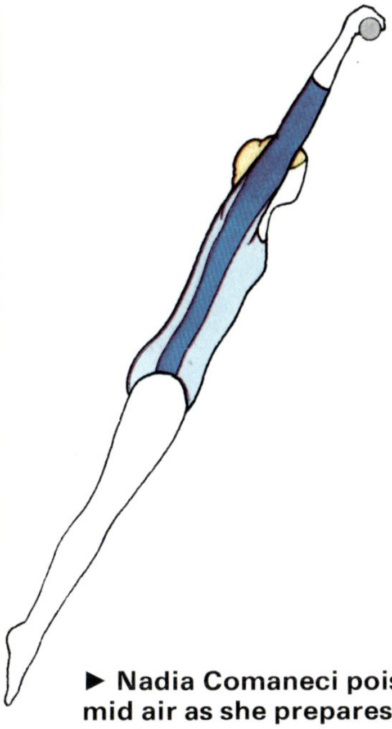

Left: The incredibly difficult and dangerous Korbut back flip.

► Nadia Comaneci poised in mid air as she prepares to land.

Although simple in nature, the early movements on the bars must be learned with the right technique under the supervision of a qualified coach.

The gymnast should take care of the hands by wearing closely fitted leather hand straps. Use adequate 'chalk'. This magnesium carbonate powder absorbs perspiration and assists the grip. Gradually the skin on the hands gets tougher, allowing longer periods of work. Do not allow the pads of skin to get too thick. They should be carefully scaled down. Rest the hands if they get too sore.

On the Beam

When the beam was first introduced, gymnasts had to perform on the bare wood. In 1975 a special non-slip padded cover was fitted so that daring tumbling moves could be done in more safety.

Since its introduction, beam work has made enormous progress. It has become an exciting spectacle with skilful linking movements between breathtaking tumbles and remarkable balance positions.

Gymnasts can lie, stand or lean over any part of the beam, but they must not touch the support legs or the floor. The beam, five metres long and ten centimetres wide, is worked at 120 cm high in major competitions, and at 110 cm in junior events. Lower, shorter beams are used for training. In training, lines on the gym floor are valuable in assessing the alignment of cartwheels, walkovers, and other

Rules for Beam

A gymnast is allowed between 70 and 90 seconds in which to complete her beam exercise. She should use the entire length of the beam and include spins, leaps, running and walking steps, at least one complete turn while moving backwards, forwards or sideways, and occasional stationary positions. Points are deducted for over-balancing, wobbling, unnecessary stops, repetition, badly linked movements or falls.

The mount, or start, can be made from a springboard. The gymnast must perform an exciting dismount, showing a controlled flight, followed by a steady landing. The entire exercise should be completely integrated and flow smoothly. As well as reaching the required degree of difficulty, the exercise should demonstrate the full range of body movement.

In competitions, the exercise begins when the gymnast's feet leave the floor or board. Five seconds before the maximum limit, a whistle is blown. After this, anything the gymnast performs is not considered.

► A well executed handstand, performed on a beam in the open air. Gymnastics displays are in demand for carnivals and galas during the summer months.

moving elements. For practising difficult tumbles, mats are placed across the beam to give protection and confidence.

There is no magic formula to help beginners stay on the beam. Leading coaches advise: learn the basic elements properly, and train long and hard; not only move straight, but think straight.

A gymnast must maintain an elegant posture on the beam. Some parts of the body should be relaxed, but most are held under tension and therefore controlled. In competitions, the code of points allocates 40 per cent (4 points) of the total score to 'execution and amplitude'. This means the way in which the exercise is performed: height of leaps, confidence level, accurate presentation and proper technique. In other words, simply 'doing' a series of movements is not enough.

Preparation

For all gymnasts, the last few moments before a competition performance are full of tension. Their nervousness shows in different ways. Some have 'butterflies' in their stomachs, others' mouths go dry. Some fidget, while others restlessly rehearse parts of their routine with arm and body movements.

Before beam and floor exercises, most gymnasts find space where they can rehearse balances and links over and over again. Then, when the gymnast's number appears on the board and the light shows green, she must concentrate all her attention on the performance ahead. This means ignoring background noise, such as applause for another performance, or another competitor's floor music.

◀ American gymnast Kathy Johnson demonstrating a box splits or side splits, a medium difficulty movement requiring precise balance.

▲ A straddle half lever, demonstrated by Nadia Comaneci. Notice the perfectly locked arms, and the height of the seat from the beam.

▲ A forward somersault on the beam. This movement needs to be performed accurately, since the landing is blind and difficult to correct.

Movements

Beginners will have difficulty in making full use of the 70 seconds allocated to the beam, as their repertoire of movements is limited. In the course of training, a coach will insist on many repetitions of walking with the head raised and eyes looking straight ahead. The coach will also encourage arms and legs to move through their full range without loss of balance. Next will come high steps, followed by leaps of differing styles, then spins and turns.

The most important aspect of beam work is the correct use of the arms. In addition, head and leg movements must be well-disciplined so that good posture is maintained at all times.

Other basic movements to be learned in the first 12 months of gymnastics include ballet movements such as the arabesque (a balance on one leg); a cartwheel dismount from the beam end; a handstand into a forward roll; a back lying push upwards into bridge (crab); squat legs through to sitting or back support; step hops and chasse steps.

The gymnast's aim on the beam should be to show a smooth, flowing and confident series of movements. Before any agility movements are tried, she should learn how to get on and off the beam, then practise standing, walking, simple balancing, running and turning.

Above: To begin with, walking on the beam is usually assisted, by holding the coach's hand. Legs, toes and arms should be fully stretched, and as soon as possible the gymnast should work on her toes.

Methods of getting on and off the beam: A leap from the springboard onto the beam end (above right). An eye for accuracy is necessary for this move requiring a running approach, a single leg take off and a landing on a 10 cm beam. The simple two-legged jump to leave the beam (right) requires the body be fully extended in mid flight. Slightly bending the legs on landing will absorb the gymnast's weight.

Below: A stride leap with change of leg into a split leap. The gymnast takes off and lands on the same leg. The legs should be horizontal in both leap and splits positions. This movement requires a high degree of skill and courage and should only be tried by an experienced gymnast.

It is likely that music will eventually accompany beam work, giving it an even closer similarity to floor work.

Left: Single leg balances. The 'Y' scale (left) is a relatively easy exercise for the young gymnast. The backward scale (right) is rated as superior in difficulty, demanding much more flexibility and a truer sense of balance. These movements are held momentarily, and should not restrict the flow of the exercise as a whole. Excessive sitting and lying positions should be avoided, although these are elements which should be shown.

The splits (left), showing two of a variety of arm positions which are optional during this movement. The hardest part of this movement is finding a smooth method of getting in and out of the position. The split leg handstand (far left) requires extreme suppleness in the back and hips.

◀ Diane Bull, a British gymnast, on the beam.

▶ Pamela Bileck of the United States performs a 'V' balance during the beam exercise at the 1984 Olympics.

Floorwork

Floorwork, more than any other exercise, is responsible for the explosion of interest in gymnastics. The magical sequences performed by leading gymnasts have captured the imaginations of millions of people around the world.

In the early stages, a girl spends much of her time mastering the basic tumbling movements and attempting simple leaps, spins and turns. As she improves, the young gymnast will try to perfect one of the graded set exercises which has a particular pattern of music to suit. She chooses elements within her capabilities, tries out the moves in various orders, adds and subtracts moves, and finally puts together an exercise that suits her style of work and her capabilities.

◀ Ecerina Szabo of Romania about to begin a floor exercise. She became Olympic champion on this apparatus at Los Angeles in 1984.

◀ Elena Moukhina, whose floor exercise included a number of difficult tumbles. Here she demonstrates a variation on the bridge position.

▲ The most famous exponent of the floor exercise, Olga Korbut.

▲ **Floor exercise should cover the entire area of the floor, and express the personality of the gymnast. In these pictures, Elena Moukhina performs an arch jump (left), and Nelli Kim a stag splits position while passing through a walkover.**

Recent developments in floor work include the introduction of graceful dance and ballet movements, an imaginative range of supple elements, and an improvement in acrobatic tumbles.

Increasingly, gimmickry has been added to floor exercises. Smaller gymnasts have used unusual spread eagle positions and tummy and seat-bouncing movements. It is likely that these unconventional elements will eventually be replaced by more orthodox gymnastics, and perhaps by exuberant dance sequences. Another fashion has been audience participation in the form of hand-clapping: a catchy piece of music accompanied by rhythmic clapping, led by team mates. No matter which direction floorwork takes, it will always be an exercise allowing the gymnast maximum self-expression.

Rules for Floorwork

Each gymnast has between 70 and 90 seconds on the specially-carpeted floor area, which measures 12 m square (40 sq. ft.). Most competitors choose the piano to accompany their performance because of its versatility and range, but a whole orchestra can be used.

The content of the exercise should cover acrobatic tumbles, leaps, spins and turns, and contain momentary pauses, showing control throughout. Exercises should include a number of movements of varying difficulty, and show virtuosity and originality. The judges take into account the way the music is interpreted. Points are lost for stumbles, loss of balance, repetitive links or a monotonous performance.

All the exercises here will at some time be performed by the best gymnasts in the world. There are hundreds of different movements, so this is not a comprehensive study. The first three show movement forward, backward and sideways. On the other page are two of the more advanced moves.

Left: A backward roll from standing. On rolling on the small of the back the palms of the hands should be facing backwards with the thumbs by the ears and the elbows tucked in. As the hands touch the mat, they lift the body off the ground.

Above: In the forward roll, the knees are bent into a squat position, and the hands placed in front of the feet to support the upper body. With the head tucked well under, the seat is raised and the roll commences.

Below: The cartwheel is an awkward movement to learn properly. The tendency is to bend the arms and legs at the wrong time and make the movement more difficult than it really is. It is best practised along a line on the gym floor.

Both the rolls and cartwheels can eventually be done on the beam. They can also be further extended into difficult, attractive combinations during a floor exercise. With a time limit of 60 or 90 seconds, a gymnast has to show her best tumbles. They must be properly integrated into the sequence, not simply strung together in a zig-zag pattern, but joined without unnecessary pauses.

Above: The handspring is one of dozens of similar agility moves learned during the first two years of a gymnast's training. The hands are dropped shoulder width in front of the feet, and the speed of the trailing leg gives the movement its lift and rotation. There is little change in the movement of the arms, as this is essentially a 'leg acting' excercise. A natural progression is to land on one leg.

◀ A gymnast halfway through a backward walkover.

Below: The forward walkover plays an important part in floor exercises. It is an advanced move, requiring extreme suppleness in the back and thighs, plus strength in the arms.

How a Competition is Organized

The organizer of a competition, whether at school or international level, is responsible for a great deal. Firstly, the venue must be chosen and booked. The facilities required vary with the level of competition. Major events need areas for first aid and administration as well as changing rooms for competitors. The site's resources, such as equipment, stewards, and catering have to be assessed. Accommodation for both gymnasts and officials must be arranged. Judges are invited by the organizer, and are vital to any competition. There are up to four for each event, plus a master judge.

The organizer's duties also include installing special equipment, such as electronic scoreboards and the public address system, advertising the event to clubs, planning and distributing publicity material, printing programmes and registering competitors.

Before the event, judges meet to discuss procedure. At an international event there are two judges from each competing nation, plus a neutral judge. Equipment is put out several hours in advance so that competitors may practise. By then, everything else in and around the arena is ready for the moment when the gymnasts march in and the competition begins.

In the two largest competitions, the Olympics and the World Championships, the gymnastics event lasts six days. During this period, everyone competes twice on each apparatus, once for the voluntary exercises (chosen by themselves) and once for the compulsory exercises (set by the F.I.G.). The top 36 then perform voluntary exercises to decide the champion. Events of this size require many additional facilities, including those for television and press coverage, security, special foods, transport, recreation facilities, decorations, ticket and souvenir sales, and much more.

This diagram shows a typical judges assesment of a top performance. The four individual judges' scores are fed into a panel at the master judge's table. The highest and the lowest of the four scores are eliminated, and the average of the remaining two displayed on the electronic scoreboard. The difference between the middle scores must not exceed 0.3 between 9.5 and 10 points, 0.5 between 8.5 and 9.45, and 1 in all other cases.

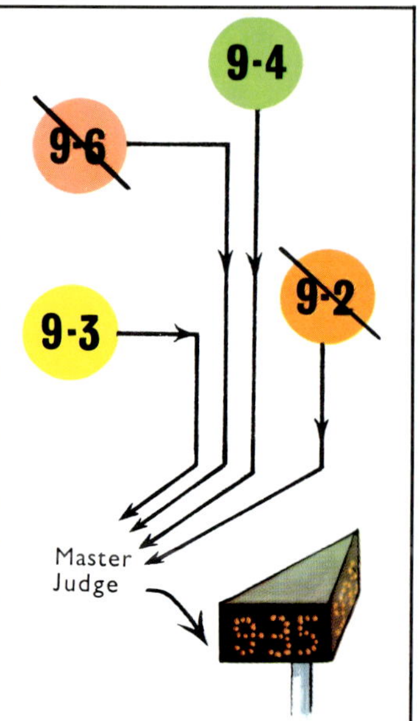

► **This layout plan is typical, although the pattern may vary. The podium (stage) stands about 90 cm high. There will always be an additional hall or large space behind the scenes for pre-competition practice and warm-up. This is a 'multi-event' layout, for both men's and women's competitions.**

◀ **The siting of equipment has to be carefully planned so that the audience can see, and the judge's view is not obstructed. There has to be space to allow for TV cameras, photographers and officials.**

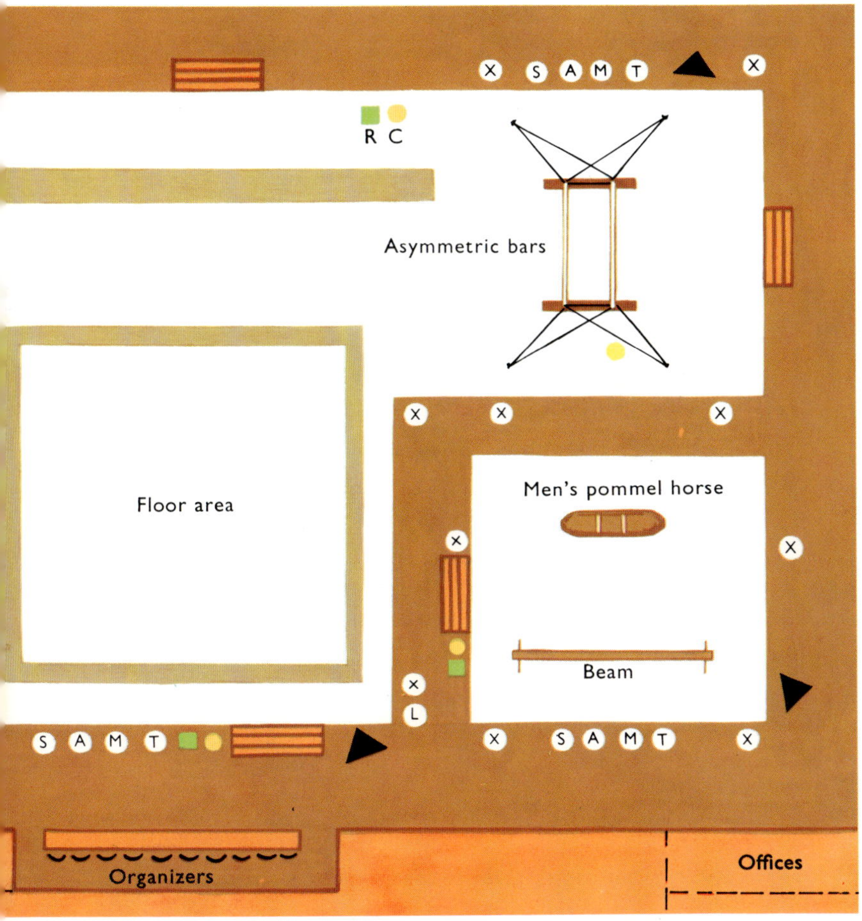

The People Involved

At the main organizer's table there are about a dozen people who are responsible for the minute-by-minute running of the competition. They are the competition director, controller, the chief scorers, announcer, officials from the organizing body, the communications steward, and at international events, interpreters.

The diagram on the left also shows other people with special duties: judges (X), the master judge (M), and his assistant (A), whose job is to sort out and collate the other judges' scores. The timekeepers (T) check the amount of warm-up time before each competition begins, and time the beam and floor exercises. Line judges (L) indicate when a competitor steps over the boundary on the floor exercises. There are scoreboard operators for the electronic scoreboards (S). At the vault, a vault steward will hold a card showing the number of the vault to be attemped. If a question mark is displayed, the vault is not listed and is original.

An electronic scoreboard (indicated by a black triangle) shows the scores for each performance. Other equipment includes trays of resin (R), used by gymnasts on their shoes to give them a firm footing, and of handchalk, used on the bars and beam. Nearby will be a damp cloth, for wiping away excess chalk.

There is always a rehearsal for all involved the week before the opening so that officials can test their arrangements and gymnasts get used to the arena, lighting and equipment.

Life at the Top

At senior international level, gymnastics is a very serious business. The gymnast's life revolves around her vital daily training sessions. She spends long hours in the gym with her coach and a small group of other gymnasts. In her diary she keeps a record of work-outs, new moves, her weight and some competition scores.

Top athletes have to control their diet, and their social life: late night parties do not mix with rigorous daily training. Few have time to enjoy other hobbies during a career which lasts, on average, eight years. Outside the gym and competition area, they must learn to accept photographers, press interviewers, curious crowds and autograph hunters.

A member of a national team is usually invited to take part in anything up to 20 international competitions each year, some at home, some abroad. Away from home, all the gymnast's expenses are paid by her national association. She wears – and afterwards keeps – the leotards, tracksuit and other official clothing provided. Handstraps and shoes,

Developing a Routine

It takes about five years for a gymnast to put together the various movements of each voluntary exercise. Her exercises will contain elements which she is particularly good at. Somebody with plenty of flexibility, for example, will include a range of moves which show her supple back and extensive range of movement in the hip girdle.

New elements are becoming increasingly difficult to find, as each coach carefully explores what can be done on each apparatus. In the search for originality, they often include moves formerly seen only in men's gymnastics.

In order to be sure that her few minutes exposure in competition are as perfect as possible, the gymnast must have the confidence that comes from constant practice and repetition.

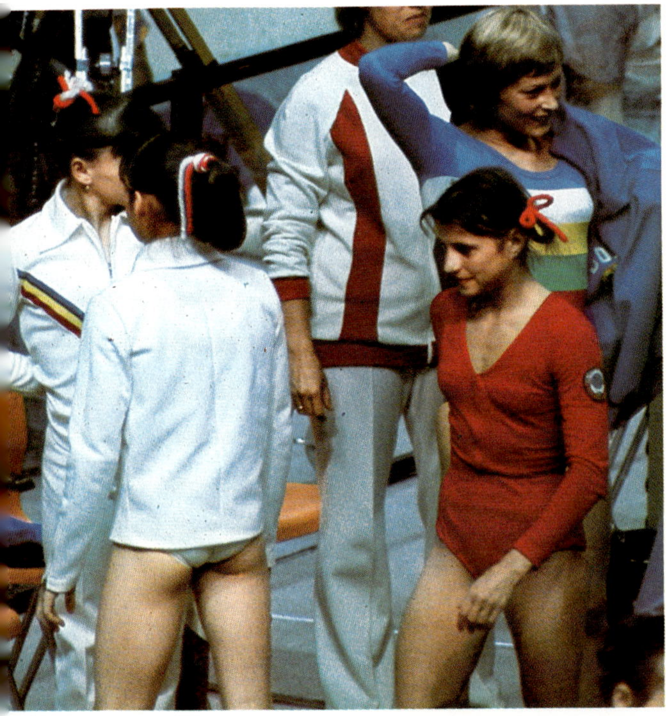

however, are usually the gymnast's own responsibility.

Invitations to championships in other countries are very popular. The trip usually lasts a week, and in addition to the challenge and excitement of the competition itself, there are the extra attractions of V.I.P. treatment and sightseeing. All host countries pay competitors a subsistence allowance for refreshment, fares, and other expenses. This is relatively small, so as not to affect amateur status. To compensate for this, gifts are often presented to visiting gymnasts.

Each gymnast is different in her mental and physical make-up. Her choice of relaxation and hours of sleep, for instance, depends entirely on her individual needs. All gymnasts, however, have one thing in common: a determination to win which makes them willing to sacrifice so many hours to what can seem monotonous repetition in search of perfection.

▲ Olga Korbut looks totally dejected as she learns she has come only fifth at the Montreal Olympics.

◄ Ludmilla Tourescheva caught in an ungainly position on the beam. There is no room for error in world competition.

► Taking the applause: jubilant 1978 World Champion Elena Moukhina of the Soviet Union.

◄ Moukhina somersaulting on the beam with the scoreboard showing her only 0.3 points behind Comaneci.

A Champion's Day

Jacqui is a champion gymnast. She is 18 years old and has just started college. Last week she returned from one international event, and next week she is off to another one.

Every day she gets up at seven o'clock. Today she straps her right ankle, which she hurt slightly during training yesterday. By half-past eight she has joined her team-mates and coach for one of two sessions. Because of her injury she avoids vault and tumbling; instead she does a lot of limbering and suppling exercises, and bar work.

After lectures and a specially prepared lunch Jacqui meets her coach in town to attend the opening of a new sports store. Then, at four, she is back in the gym for her second training session. Later, she has her ankle treated by a physiotherapist, then goes home, watches TV for a while – and is early to bed.

Championships

The three most important events in the international gymnastic calendar are the Olympic Games, the World Championships and the European championships.

▶ Emilia Eberle of Romania seen here on the bars during the European Championship in 1979, performing a daring cross hand change while in the inverted straddle position.

European Championships

Because the European Championships have always included East European competitors, they are as important an event as the World Championships themselves.

The competition lasts two days, although competitors generally spend about a week at the site. The first day's competition is to decide the overall champion. It consists of eight groups of eight or nine gymnasts performing in two rounds. On the second day, the top eight perform to decide the champion for each apparatus.

World Championships

The World Championships involve nearly thirty groups of six gymnasts in both the men's and women's sections, from a total of seventy countries.

On the first four days, men's and women's events alternate from day to day. The fifth day is for the top 36 competitors, and the last day for the finalists. Two days of celebrations follow the end of the championships.

▶ Nelli Kim on the beam, preparing to land from a split leap.

◀ Kathy Johnson taking up her characteristic starting pose for the floor exercise, familiar from several championships in the late 1970s.

European Champions

	Champion	Vault	Asymmetric bars	Beam	Floor
1973	Tourescheva (USSR)	Tourescheva (USSR)	Tourescheva (USSR)	Tourescheva (USSR)	Tourescheva (USSR)
1975	Comaneci (Romania)	Comaneci (Romania)	Comaneci (Romania)	Comaneci (Romania)	Kim (USSR)
1977	Comaneci (Romania)	Kim (USSR)	Comaneci (Rom) Moukhina (USSR)	Moukhina (USSR)	Moukhina (USSR) Filatova (USSR)
1979	Comaneci (Romania)	Comaneci (Romania)	Moukhina (USSR)	Shaposhnikova (USSR)	Comaneci (Romania)
1981	Gnank (E. Germany)	Grigoras (Romania)	Gnank (E. Germany)	Gnank (E. Germany)	Gnank (E. Germany)
1983	Bicherova (USSR)	Bicherova (USSR)	Szabo (Romania)	Agache (Romania)	Bicherova USSR Szabo (Rom)

World Champions

	Team	Champion	Vault	Asymmetric bars	Beam	Floor
1970	USSR	Tourescheva (USSR)	Zuchold (E. Germany)	Janz (W. Germany)	Zuchold (E. Germany)	Tourescheva (USSR)
1974	USSR	Tourescheva (USSR)	Korbut (USSR)	Zinke (W. Germany)	Tourescheva (USSR)	Tourescheva (USSR)
1978	USSR	Moukhina (USSR)	Comaneci (Romania)	Frederick (USA)	Comaneci (Romania)	Comaneci (Romania)
1979	Romania	Kim (USSR)	Kim (USSR)	Ma (China)	Cerna (Czech)	Eberle (Romania)
1981	USSR	Bicherova (USSR)	Gnank (E. Germany)	Gnank (E. Germany)	Gnank (E. Germany)	Ilienko (USSR)
1983	USSR	Urichenko (USSR)	Stoyanova (Bulgaria)	Gnank (E. Germany)	Mostepanova (USSR)	Szabo (Romania)

The Olympics

Every young gymnast's ultimate ambition is to be selected to compete in the Olympic Games. It was not until 1928 that women were first allowed to take part in gymnastics events. The individual events were introduced in 1952. The impact that the women gymnasts have made has been astonishing.

A girl who represents her country in one Olympiad will have been fortunate. Several have managed to stay at the top long enough to take part in two, but only rarely three Olympiads.

There are many qualifying trials and much anxious waiting, before a gymnast is told that she is to be included in the Olympic squad. From this squad, the final team will be selected by the coach and manager. This selection is, however made at the site only a week before the event.

Teams are taken to the Olympic Village, where they will spend up to five weeks isolated from press and public. Training schedules have to be rigidly adhered to, for transport and training facilities have to be allocated

▲ **Nelli Kim of the Soviet Union delighted audiences at international competitions for several years during the late 1970s. Her floor work and vaults were outstanding, and she was only the second gymnast in the history of the Olympics to achieve the magic score of 10 points.**

◀ **Vera Caslavska of Czechoslovakia in the middle of her split leg hollow back somersault in the floor exercise. She won the gold medal on this piece at Mexico in 1968.**

Olympic Champions

	Team	Champion	Vault	Asymmetric bars	Beam	Floor
1956	USSR	Latynina (USSR)	Latynina (USSR)	Keleti (Hungary)	Keleti (Hungary)	Keleti (Hun) Latynina (USSR)
1960	USSR	Latynina (USSR)	Nikolajeva (USSR)	Astkhova (USSR)	Bosakova (Czech)	Latynina (USSR)
1964	USSR	Caslavska (Czech)	Caslavska (Czech)	Caslavska (Czech)	Caslavska (Czech)	Latynina (USSR)
1968	USSR	Caslavska (Czech)	Caslavska (Czech)	Caslavska (Czech)	Kutchinskaya (USSR)	Caslavska (Cz) Petrik (USSR)
1972	USSR	Tourescheva (USSR)	Janz (W. Germany)	Janz (W. Germany)	Korbut (USSR)	Korbut (USSR)
1976	USSR	Comaneci (Romania)	Kim (USSR)	Comaneci (Romania)	Comaneci (Romania)	Kim (USSR)
1980	USSR	Davidova (USSR)	Shaposhnikova (USSR)	Gnank (E. Germany)	Comaneci (Romania)	Kim (USSR) Comaneci (Rom)
1984	Romania	Retton (USA)	Szabo (Romania)	Ma (China)	Pauca (Romania)	Szabo (Romania)

evenly between teams. Three- or four-hour sessions, twice daily, are timetabled for each country, so work may start early and finish late.

Coaches will insist on rigorous training sessions. The team will go through each of the eight complete exercises many, many times. They concentrate on parts that are weak, and make occasional alterations when they see other teams' interpretations.

Each day is divided between men's and women's events, starting early in the morning and continuing through the day and into the evening. All competitors are free to enter their own competition hall and watch others, and to watch other sports as well. This is marvellous for the gymnasts, who, can relax and watch the rest of the Olympic programme, until they join the closing cermony.

► Lavina Agache of Romania helps her team to a score of 392.20 to beat the host nation and win the team championships at the Los Angeles Olympics.

Great Gymnasts

Today's massive interest in artistic gymnastics is due largely to the personalities of individual performers. Here, there is only room to highlight the achievements of a few of these dynamic sportswomen.

Ludmilla Tourescheva
Ludmilla Tourescheva dominated women's international events during the 1970s. Her classically correct approach to gymnastics gained her many all-round and individual titles; but despite her success, she was overshadowed in popular appeal by Korbut and Comaneci.

Kathy Johnson
By her precise use of straight arm work, the American Kathy Johnson brought a new dimension to asymmetric bar exercises. She also excelled at floor exercises, where she combined serene movements with crisp, high tumbling links.

Larissa Latynina
Perhaps one of the greatest gymnasts of all time, Larissa Latynina is now the coach to the Soviet women's team. She brought charm, skill and beauty to what was a powerful, masculine-orientated sport, winning 24 gold medals at Olympic, World and European championships. She retired shortly after the 1964 Tokyo Olympiad.

▼ Nadia Comaneci concentrates at the end of the vault runway, preparing herself for another astonishing vault.

▼ The tiny Maria Filatova of the Soviet Union, whose small size made extra demands on her skill.

◄ Olga Korbut in her best-known exercise, the floor.

▼ The champions' rostrum at the 1976 Montreal Olympics, and three of the world's most successful gymnasts. Nadia Comaneci became the youngest ever Olympic Champion at the age of 14. Nelli Kim took the silver medal, and the veteran Ludmilla Tourescheva the bronze.

▲ Kathy Johnson, the overall American champion in 1979, seen here in her best exercise, the floor. Her distinctive striped leotard became a personal trade mark.

Nadia Comaneci
Fourteen year-old Nadia Comaneci from Romania set the Montreal Olympics alight by giving the most breathtaking performance ever seen in women's gymnastics. Before becoming the youngest Olympic champion in history, Nadia Comaneci had been European champion at the age of 13. She was spotted at school at the age of only six, and was trained and encouraged by Bela Karoly, Romania's leading coach.

Vera Caslavska
The style and personality of the Czech, Vera Caslavska, greatly affected the development of the sport in the decade 1959–1968. Her superlative work marked a significant turning-point in women's gymnastics. Altogether she won 22 World, Olympic and European titles despite the fact that she was already 22 years old when she took her first Olympic medals at Tokyo in 1964.

Olga Korbut
Olga Korbut's glowing personality stole the limelight at every event in which she participated. She was also a truly great gymnast. At the Munich Olympics she made history by including a standing back somersault in her routine, and won the gold medal. This daring somersault had never been performed before and created quite a storm; in fact it almost led to ban of such dangerous tumbles on beam.

Avril Lennox
Avril Lennox was one of Britain's best gymnasts. She was overall British champion for four consecutive years, and took part in 105 major competitions, including two Olympic Games, one World and three European Championships.

Glossary of Exercises

Key V: Vault; AB: Asymmetric bars; B: Beam; FX: Floor exercises.

Aerial Cartwheel A cartwheel without using the hands. Thrusting hard from one leg, half turn to land on the opposite leg (B, FX).
Back Uprise A method of moving from hanging below the bar to support (AB).
Beat Swing In hang or support, the legs swing backwards from a half piked position to create a whip swing action in preparation for the next move (AB).
Bridge or **Crab** A backward bend. The arched body is supported by the hands and feet (B, FX).
Chasse A step in which one foot remains in front of the other (B, FX).
Cossack Steps Kicking steps taken from a squat position (B, FX).
Eagle swings or **dislocation** With arms slightly wider than shoulders, the top bar is caught behind the gymnast with hands in cubital grasp (AB).
Extension The stretching of the body or part of the body to its furthest extent.
First Flight The short space of time between take-off and contact with the apparatus.
Flank vault Taken over the bar, beam or horse with the side of the body downwards, being supported on one arm.
Gainer back somersault A back somersault performed while running forwards (B, FX).
Glide A controlled swing of the body, passing smoothly from one point to another; for example, the swing of a long upstart on the bars.
Half seat circle The piked body sinks backwards or forwards on the straight arms to below the bar (AB)
Hang When the body is suspended below the equipment, held by the hands.
Hecht A straight body dismount from the asymmetric bars done from a backward hip circle or a long swing.
Hip Beat or **Cast** From front support, the back is rounded as legs come forwards, and from a slightly bent arm, the legs swing vigorously backwards to a final position with the extended body above the bar on straight arms (AB).
Lay out From a support position on the top bar, the legs swing backwards as the arms and body are fully extended into a horizontal position, to continue a powerful downward swing (AB).
Mill circle A complete circle in the straddle support position (AB).
Mixed grasp One hand in over grasp and one hand in under grasp (AB).
Mount The first move or start to an exercise, used for getting on to the beam and bars.

▼ Moukhina demonstrates a variation on the bridge, passing through the position which normally shows legs together.

▶ **Nadia Comaneci in a steady straddle half lever at the 1978 World Championships (left). Susan Cheesebrough of Great Britain passing through a piked hang on the bars (far left).**

Neck spring From a momentary support position on the neck and the back of the head, the legs whip over from the piked body and the arms push away from the horse top or floor to a standing position (V, FX).
Needle scale A balance on one foot with the other leg extended upwards and backwards (B, FX).
Paces Steps or strides before a movement or mount.
Pike A position produced by raising the extended legs towards the trunk.
Pirouette A spin of the body in the vertical plane, either upright or in the handstand position.
Pre-flight The brief moment before the feet leave the springboard and before the first flight onto the horse occurs. (V).
Radochla Somersault A somersault from low bar to high bar with legs straddled, re-grasping the top bar with hands between the legs. Named after an East German gymnast (AB).
Reverse Hang Feet between the hands until legs and body are fully stretched below (AB).
Rotation A turn around an axis (an imaginary line) or around the apparatus, having a circular motion.
Routine Another name for a gymnastic exercise.
Scale A balancing pose performed on one leg.
Sheep vault A simple vault in which the bent knees pass between the hands (V).
Squat The knees and hips are bent with the seat near to the heels.
Straddle half lever Supported on hands and straight arms, the gymnast lifts the seat while the legs are spread wide and level with the ground or beam.
Take off The point after contact with the springboard, and before the pre-flight (V).
Tsukahara A vault consisting of a cartwheel and a back somersault from the hands.
Tuck When the legs are bent close to the chest, as in a somersault.
Twist A turn about the vertical axis.
Vertical astride vault The gymnast vaults in an upright position with the legs spread downwards and sideways, pressing both hands firmly on the horse.
Walkover A movement in which the body passes forward or backward through a split handstand. A free walkover is one without the use of the hands (B, FX).
'Y' scale Standing on one leg, with the other held high and to the side (B, FX).

Index

Acknowledgements

Photographs: Allsport (Tony Duffy) page 9 *top*, 10 *top*, 11 *top and bottom*, 16 *bottom left*, 17 *top*, 20 *right*, 21 *centre*, 24 *bottom*, 25 *left and right*, 32, 34, 35, 37 *top right*, 38 *right*; Allsport (Don Morley) 16 *top*, 17 *bottom right*, 31 *top*; Allsport/Photographic Ltd 17 *bottom left*, 37 *bottom*; Allsport (Steve Powell) 4; Colorsport cover, 1, 16 *top*, 23 *right*, 24 *top*, 31 *bottom*, 35 *bottom*, *top centre*; E. D. Lacey 16 *right*, 30 *top*, 36 *bottom*; Mansell Collection 6 *centre*; Peter Moeller 5, 10 *bottom*, 23, 31; Novosti 28 *right*, 36 *right*; Popper Photos 8 *top*; Radio Times Hulton Picture Library 7 *centre*; G. R. Roberts 9 *bottom*; SAM 8 *bottom*, 12 *right*, 30 *bottom*; Sporting Pictures (UK) Ltd 11 *centre*, 20 *top*, *21 right*, 36 *top*; S & G Press Agency 18, 19.